BABY BOWL

Also by Kim McCosker

4 Ingredients Christmas: Recipes for a Simply Yummy Holiday

By Kim McCosker and Rachael Bermingham

4 Ingredients

4 Ingredients Gluten-Free

BABY BOWL

Home-Cooked Meals for Happy, Healthy Babies and Toddlers

Kim McCosker

ATRIA PAPERBACK

New York London Toronto Sydney New Delhi

ATRIA PAPERBACK

A Division of Simon & Schuster, Inc.
1230 Avenue of the Americas
New York, NY 10020

First Atria Paperback edition October 2012

ATRIA PAPERBACK and colophon are trademarks of Simon & Schuster, Inc.

For more information about special discounts for bulk purchases,
please contact Simon & Schuster Special Sales at
1-866-506-1949 or business@simonandschuster.com.

The Simon & Schuster Speakers Bureau can bring authors
to your live event. For more information or to book an event,
contact the Simon & Schuster Speakers Bureau at
1-866-248-3049 or visit our website at www.simonspeakers.com.

Baby Blocks font created by Ryan D. Neaveill

Manufactured in the United States of America

10 9 8 7 6 5 4 3 2 1

Library of Congress Cataloging-in-Publication Data
McCosker, Kim.
    Baby bowl : home-cooked meals for happy, healthy babies and toddlers / Kim McCosker.
    1. Baby foods.   2. Infants—Nutrition.   3. Toddlers—Nutrition.   I. Title.
    TX740.M344   2012
    641.3'00832—dc23   2012029449

ISBN 978-1-4516-7809-3
ISBN 978-1-4516-7810-9 (ebook)

TO MY BOYS,

Glen, Morgan,

Hamilton, and Flynn

You are my reasons for being.

Anton Avocado
is a fruit, not a vegetable. Avocados have the highest protein content of any fruit.

Archie Apple
What's the old saying? "An apple a day keeps the doctor away." Yet the average person eats only 65 apples a year . . . oops!

Baby Blueberry
Blueberries are incredibly high in antioxidants and are often referred to as the "brainberry."

Bella Banana
offers a great source of dietary fiber. So easy to prepare: simply peel, mash, and enjoy.

Benny Broccoli
Super nutritious. High in Vitamin C and folic acid.

Carrie Carrot
Always in season. Nutrient-dense, containing enzymes and minerals.

Sally Squash
Her vibrant orange color is a dead giveaway to the power of squash. She's packed with nutrients.

Pierre Potato
The potato was the first-ever food grown in space, in 1995. Potatoes are rich in complex carbohydrates that can supply energy for growing bodies.

CONTENTS

NOTE

Where it is necessary to use "he" or "she" in reference to the baby, I have used "he." This reflects only the fact that I have cooked for and fed three baby boys!

The baby must know that he is a miracle,
that since the beginning of the world there hasn't been,
and until the end of the world there will not be,
another like him.

—*Pablo Casals,*
Spanish composer, cellist, and conductor

BABY BOWL

INTRODUCTION

Well, hello there! I am so very glad *Baby Bowl* has made it into your hands. Perhaps it has found you because you are expecting a baby, have one already, or know someone with her own baby on the way. Whatever your interest, *Baby Bowl* was written to help you navigate baby's "menus" amid what is often a blur of late nights and early mornings in a cocoon of love. Ah, motherhood—the most demanding role I have ever undertaken—but the one I want to succeed at the most.

My name is Kim McCosker. I am a mother, wife, daughter, granddaughter, sister, auntie, cousin, and friend. I believe the heart of all homes is smack-bang in the kitchen. My hometown is Mundubbera, a small country town in Queensland. There were no twenty-four-hour grocery stores and any money that came our way was plowed (literally) straight back into our farm—it was not to be wasted. So my beautiful mum learned to be very creative in the kitchen, making wonderful meals from minimal ingredients. Her mum, my grandmother, a widow way too early with four kids, was the same. I learned to cook from them, so to me, food means family. My mum and grandmother made the dinner table a place to connect and communicate. It was a fun place where my brothers and I would try to create ways to get rid of peas other than by eating them (gross!). And so it is today in my house, although a lot, lot messier with my three boys (and it's not the peas they're protesting about, it's the cauliflower and beets).

I have a degree in international finance; I'm an author and a businesswoman. I'd *like* to play golf more, help in my boys' classrooms more often, and read the paper from start to finish just once this year. I am a really busy person who works my life and schedule around my family. I juggle many balls on any given day, doing the best I know how, sometimes successfully, sometimes dreadfully! But above all, *I am just like you*—a proud parent wanting to learn how to start on the right path to feeding their baby.

You may know the 4 Ingredients series I put together with my coauthor Rachael Bermingham. Actually, this book grew out of those. On tours around Australia in 2008 and 2009, doing lots and lots of author talks in hundreds of libraries, I would always ask the librarians, "What books are you regularly asked for?" The reply was often, "A baby food book." What a great idea, I thought, and now here it is!

Baby Bowl differs from 4 Ingredients in an important way—many of these recipes have way more than four ingredients in them. "Why?" you may ask. Because, Mum and Dad, this is your moment! A stellar opportunity to offer your beautiful little babies as many vegetables and as much fruit and combinations of both as their little bellies will hold. This is the time your little angels are willing to try anything. Wait till they turn three, and the very minestrone soup they loved yesterday they completely reject today "because it's got that green stuff in it!" "What green stuff?" you ask, astonished. Oh—vegetables!

When my boys were babies, I wouldn't serve dinner without at least four vegetables cooked, baked, or mashed into it. So there was my "4 ingredients" quota gone in one food group!

The recipes in *Baby Bowl* are simple, healthy ideas aimed at introducing as many flavors to your baby's palate as possible, before it turns into the psychotic personality it may later become (the palate, that is!). They were developed to include the goodness of each food group along with their five veggies and two fruits a day.

I have been blessed with three absolutely beautiful boys, and no amount of reading or research could have prepared me for the reality of motherhood and the enormous responsibility that accompanies it. There is so much information available these days, and for the advice of every expert another will tell you why it's wrong! I wrote this book based on what worked for me, on advice passed from my grandmother to my mother and now to me. And guess what? With this simple gift of good nutritional sense, I have managed to raise three happy, healthy boys. (Say a prayer that this now continues!) And if I can do it, anyone can.

Where do you start when introducing solids to your baby?

With *Baby Bowl*—a practical, easy cookbook
written by one loving mum for others.

With love & nourishment,

Kim

FOOD FOR LIFE

t's an astonishing fact that a newborn baby will triple its birth weight in the first year of his little life. This growth is only possible because of the milk he is drinking and the food he is eating. The milk and food you give him build a bigger baby.

The type and quality of food we offer our baby in his first year of life is vitally important. Research indicates that the best time to introduce solids is at about six months of age. Naturally, some babies and circumstances will dictate a different approach, but for the purpose of this book I have assumed that your little bundle of joy is about six months of age when you're introducing solids.

This is an important turning point, because neither breast milk nor formula alone can provide your baby with enough nutrients, particularly iron, once he reaches six months. The iron stores your baby built up before birth will have diminished. So introducing your baby to solid foods at this age is a crucial part of his development.

Disclaimer
Every effort has been made to ensure that these recipes are as appropriate as possible for your precious baby. But each baby is different. If you have any concerns about diet or any other issue, talk to your family doctor, pediatrician, or dietitian.

Handy Kitchen Tools for Making Baby Food

As a mum of three beautiful boys (okay, I'm biased), one of the best tips I can offer you is to cook in bulk for your baby. It saves so much angst on busy days, or days when you are just plain exhausted, if you can simply pull something yummy from your freezer for your baby's bowl.

But first, you need some basic equipment. From baby's first purees to more advanced meals, having handy kitchen tools at your disposal makes baby food preparation quick and easy.

Here is a simple list I found invaluable when I was the pureeing purist.

- Mini blender or food processor.
- Stick blender, for a quick puree.
- Storage containers with lids. I have seen ice cube trays with lids that are ideal.
- Individual plastic storage containers are great for storage, freezing, and thawing.
- Peeler.
- Colander.
- Silicone mini muffin pan.
- Knife and cutting board.
- Kitchen scale.

What I Learned When Starting Out

To be honest, I don't think it dawned on me until my third child—which is odd, as I have a finance degree from college—but the trick with introducing solids is to approach feeding as a "joint venture" between you and your baby. You decide what food to prepare, and your baby decides how much of it to eat. Easy, right?

When starting out, here are a few tips I found *extremely* helpful in keeping my sanity in check.

Top Tips

1. Follow your gut instinct. Offering your baby good, nutritious food doesn't have to be expensive or complicated; a little imagination goes a long way.

2. Go into this with patience and a sense of humor. Try and be relaxed about the whole process.

3. Learn to tolerate mess and chaos. Don't exclude your baby from eating with the family just because he will hurl food everywhere and rub it in his hair, ears, and eyes. He is a little sponge, soaking up everything, and will soon learn that this is where we eat—we hope!

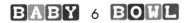

Baby Food Preparation

There are four basic cooking methods, and you are probably familiar with all of them.

1. **Steaming:** Generally speaking, this is the best way to retain nutrients. If you don't have an electric steamer, simply place the food in a colander over a pan of boiling water.

2. **Boiling:** This is also a great way to prepare baby's first foods, so long as you don't boil the life out of them. If you boil, do so with a minimal amount of water and preferably in a saucepan with a glass lid. Lifting the lid as food boils releases nutrients. Keep any remaining liquid when you're done, to thin purees if necessary.

3. **Baking:** There's nothing like the natural sweetness of squash or sweet potato baked in its skin, then scraped out.

4. **Microwaving:** Some people love using their microwave and others don't. If you are one of the latter, then you will prefer the preparation methods above. If you're like me and do use your microwave, then that's fine, too. It has been said that using a microwave to prepare baby's first foods actually helps preserve the nutrients within, as food tends to cook quickly and with little water.

If you can manage to cook in bulk, you can prepare an entire month's supply of food in one afternoon. Many of baby's first foods will be okay to freeze and thaw within a month. Just remember to use a tray that has a lid, to prevent freezer burn (when ice crystals form and moisture within evaporates, leaving the food dried out).

Baby Food Storage

Use this table as a basic guideline, and label containers so you know how long they've been stored.

FOOD TYPE	FRIDGE	FREEZER
Egg yolks	1 day	1–2 months
Meat	1 day	1–2 months
Meat-vegetable combination	1–2 days	1–2 months
Cooked fruits and vegetables	2–3 days	1–3 months

Remember, frozen foods that are kept too long may look all right, but they will have lost some of their flavor and nutritional value.

Thawing and Preparing Frozen Food

- Each evening, select from the freezer the foods you plan to give your baby the next day.

- Place in the refrigerator to thaw (this usually takes at least three or four hours).

- Fruit will not need to be warmed before use.

- To warm other food, use an electric warming dish, heat the foods in a dish over boiling water, or use a microwave.

- In all cases, stir the food thoroughly and test before serving to ensure the temperature is pleasant and safe.

- *Always* throw away any leftover reheated food. Freezing foods causes some cell damage as ice crystals expand in the food, which means that frozen foods deteriorate faster than fresh.

- All thawed food should be used within 48 hours, and 24 hours for meat, fish, or egg yolk.

Offering Food to Baby

To be honest, I approached weaning my first child with a great deal of trepidation. I was more nervous about it than when I took my SATs! Had I read enough? Did I know exactly what foods to begin with? How did I store them? What if he didn't like them? I was so cautious about varying foods I cleaned my local produce market out of squash in the first month!

Thankfully, Morgan didn't turn orange, and when my mum asked, "What else are you giving him?" I thought: *Oh! Perhaps I should expand my repertoire!*

**Here begins a feeding frenzy that will last you approximately 25,732 breakfasts, lunches, and dinners.
The average age a child leaves home these days is 24.
Great—only another 23½ years to go!**

Initially, try offering your baby small amounts of food on the end of a soft, shallow baby spoon. If your baby refuses to eat, *don't worry*. Try again in a couple of days. As a guide:

• Rice cereal and fruits and vegetables separately first (see "Six Months")

• Offer solids once a day for the first week

• Twice a day for the second week

• Three times a day in the third week

For further guidance, see the baby menu planners on pages 132 to 139.

Extra meals can be added once the first meal is being taken well and enjoyed. Some babies progress to three meals a day quickly, while others take many weeks.

If you want the recipes containing formula to be lactose-free, simply substitute with lactose-free formula.

The Importance of Nutrition

We've all heard the expression "You are what you eat." Well, this extends to babies, too. Babies' growth and development are optimized when the following nutrients are included in their diets.

Protein	Chicken, peas, lentils, almond meal, eggs, milk, cheese, yogurt, baked beans, peanut butter
Essential Fats	Chicken, tuna, flaxseed, whole grains, sunflower seeds, avocado, nuts, corn, butter
Complex Carbohydrates	Banana, potato, whole-grain bread, rice, pasta, rolled oats

Vitamins & Minerals

Vitamin A	Carrots, eggs, chicken, peas, spinach, winter squash, tomato
Vitamin B groups	Brown rice, barley, oats, chicken, red meat, spinach, broccoli, mushrooms, corn
Vitamin C	Berries, mango, tomato, potato, kiwi fruit, pears, oranges, watermelon, winter squash, apple, broccoli, cauliflower, peaches, peas, raisins, red bell pepper

Vitamin D	Eggs, bell pepper, sweet potato, tuna, fish, cheese, milk
Calcium	Brown rice, spinach, raspberries, winter squash, cheese, milk, broccoli, cauliflower, peas, lentils, oats, almond meal, sesame seeds, tofu
Iodine	Spinach, milk, cheese, yogurt, banana, tuna
Iron	Egg yolk, apricots, brown rice, spinach, winter squash, plums, prunes, tuna, chicken, parsnip, lentils, corn, raisins, golden raisins, lamb, millet, avocado, banana, broccoli, peas, rolled oats
Magnesium	Brown rice, spinach, winter squash, broccoli, cauliflower, peas, lentils, corn, oats, almond meal, carrot
Selenium	Tuna, sesame seeds, tomatoes, broccoli, wheat germ
Zinc	Eggs, peas, lamb, sunflower seeds, brown rice, almond meal, cucumber, cauliflower, chicken

The Importance of Homemade Baby Food

The ingredients of many commercially made baby foods have been heated to high temperatures before cooling to sterilize and prolong shelf life. This process destroys not only a lot of flavor in the meals but many of the nutrients.

Raw fruits like apples, avocados, bananas, cherimoyas, papayas, and cantaloupe are more nutritious than cooked ones, as none of the nutrients have been lost.

There is no healthier way to feed your baby than by making food for him yourself. You will know exactly what food is going into his little body to fuel his rapid and remarkable growth.

FOODS TO TRY & WHEN

(Feel free to copy this page and stick it on the fridge for easy reference)

	6–8 months	8–10 months	10–12 months	12+ months

Cereal & grain	Farina
	Oats
	Rice
		Baby muesli
		Barley
		Lentils
		Polenta
			Arrowroot &
			  multigrain
			  biscuits
			Flaxmeal
			Quinoa pasta
			Toast	

Fruit	Apples Apricots Avocado Bananas Mango Peaches Pears Melons	Cherries Nectarines Plums Prunes	Blueberries Dates Figs Grapes Kiwifruit Papaya Tomatoes	Citrus Strawberries
Vegetables	Broccoli Carrot Green Beans Parsnip Potato Pumpkin Rutabaga Sweet potato	Cauliflower Celery Corn Leek Peas Zucchini	Asparagus Bell pepper Broccoli Cabbage Eggplant Mushrooms Onions	
Protein	Chicken	Bacon Beef Ground meat Lamb Turkey	Baked beans Kidney beans Fish Ham Pork Salmon	Eggs

Dairy		Cheddar cheese
		Tofu
		Yogurt
			Cheese:
			  cottage
			  cream
			  Parmesan
			  ricotta	

Colorful, natural foods = plenty of natural, healthy goodness.

ALLERGIES

What Is an Allergy?

The term "allergen" comes from two Greek words: *alos* (other) and *argon* (action). An allergy is an adverse reaction from the body to an allergen—foreign material. Antibodies are produced and cause the allergic reaction. Acting as the body's army, antibodies are proteins generally found in the blood that detect and destroy invaders, such as bacteria and viruses.

The greatest incidence of allergic reactions to food occurs in the first few years of life. There is no need to be overly worried unless there is a history of allergies such as hay fever, asthma, or eczema in your family.

Food allergies affect about one in thirteen U.S. children. Interestingly, 90 percent of all food-allergic reactions in the United States are caused by just eight foods.[1] These are:

- Milk
- Egg
- Peanut
- Tree nuts (walnut, cashew, etc.)
- Fish
- Shellfish
- Soy
- Wheat

[1] http://yourlife.usatoday.com/fitness-food/safety/story/2011/06/Study-says-1-in-13-US-children
-have-food-allergy/48646256/1
http://www.kidswithfoodallergies.org/resourcespre.php?id=107

Common Symptoms of Allergies

- Abdominal cramps
- Itching
- Swelling (lips, eyes, etc.)
- Rash
- Hives
- Vomiting
- Diarrhea
- Excessive mucus
- Anaphylaxis*

*An extreme, often life-threatening, allergic reaction to an antigen (e.g., a bee sting) to which the body has become hypersensitive. It must be treated *immediately*.

What Is an Intolerance?

An intolerance is an adverse reaction to food without the production of antibodies.

Food intolerance reactions have the same symptoms as allergies, but may also involve the following:

- Respiratory system (stuffy or runny nose, asthma, frequent colds and infections)

- Gastrointestinal tract (irritable bowel symptoms, colic, bloating, diarrhea, vomiting, frequent mouth ulcers, reflux, bedwetting)

- Central nervous system (migraines, headaches, anxiety, depression, lethargy, impairment of memory and concentration, panic attacks, irritability, restlessness, inattention, sleep disturbance, restless legs, mood swings)

Foods to Avoid or Be Wary Of in Baby's First 12 Months

Additives & Colorings
Another great reason to make food at home, so you know exactly what it contains

Excessive Sugar
Passes immediately into the bloodstream giving quick but unnatural energy bursts

Eggs
May contain salmonella, which is a food-poisoning bacteria

Fish & Shellfish
Orange roughy, shark, tilefish, marlin, and swordfish have higher levels of mercury than other fish

Honey
May contain botulism spores, which can cause illness or death

Peanuts
In a small number of children, peanuts trigger a nut allergy, which can be long-lasting and very serious.

Sesame Seeds
The food allergen awareness program of the Food & Drug Administration (FDA) consists of eight common foods that cause the serious allergic reactions listed on page 16. It's interesting to note that Australia, Canada, and the European Commission

include sesame in their lists of major allergy-causing substances, but in the United States, the allergen hasn't made the cut. It should still be brought to people's attention, as eating habits expand and more foods are introduced into everyday diets.[2] It is the protein found in sesame seeds that causes a reaction.

Wheat

Wheat intolerance is more common than wheat allergy and can cause quite severe gut reactions. Although allergies may be outgrown, intolerances to certain foods are usually lifelong, so the troublesome food has to be permanently avoided.

This list is a general guideline and should not be considered definitive. Always consult your healthcare professional with any concerns. Please see the Resources section on page 140 for useful contacts.

2 http://www.kidswithfoodallergies.org/resourcespre.php?id=107

	Egg-free
	Gluten-free
	Lactose-free
	Vegetarian
	Freezable

HYGIENE

Due to their developing immune systems and small body size, babies are at a greater risk than adults of illness from bacteria in food, which is mainly caused by incorrectly stored and handled foods.

Bacteria grows in temperatures between 40° and 140°F. It is generally accepted that food left at room temperature for more than two hours is considered to have been in the "danger zone" long enough for bacteria to develop. Room temperature is considered to be about 68°F, though, so if you live in a warm climate, be even more cautious.

Remember the old adage:
"If in doubt, throw it out!"

Storing Food

When storing food for later use, it is important to cool it quickly. Divide a large portion into smaller amounts to create faster cooling times.

Hot food in small containers can be placed into the freezer right away; just ensure the food is well sealed.

In the Fridge

The temperature in the door compartments of the fridge is generally not as cold as the main section of the refrigerator, so be careful about what you store in the door.

As a precautionary measure, store cooked foods away from raw foods to prevent cross-contamination.

In the Freezer

Food stored in the freezer has a limited life, too. Certain bacteria can grow in the cold, although over a longer period of time.

Freeze foods for babies of six to nine months in ice cube trays (preferably with a cover) and for older children in quarter- and half-cup containers; this allows for less waste and quicker thawing. See Baby Food Storage on page 8 for recommended freezing times and further information.

REFLUX

What Is Reflux?

Reflux is a condition where the contents of the stomach flow back into the esophagus, causing discomfort or pain. A more complicated form of the condition is Pediatric Gastroesophageal Reflux Disease (or Pediatric GERD).

I've known plenty of parents of children who suffer from reflux and seen just how hard it was for them to determine what the problem was and how best to deal with it. Some estimates say that up to half of all babies are born with some degree of infant reflux. Unfortunately, it is often misdiagnosed as colic. This can mean that many miserable months may go by before some babies receive the treatment or simple feeding modifications they need.

Look out for these symptoms if your baby is unsettled, and please see your doctor with any concerns about feeding or health. Remember to trust a "mother's instinct."

Symptoms of Infant Reflux

Some of these can be very like colic.

- Frequent crying—sometimes persistent, sometimes sudden
- Vomiting or spitting up
- Irritability
- Arching of back or neck during or after feeds
- Frequent hiccups
- Frequent waking, or the inability to sleep for long periods
- Frequent ear infections

Symptoms of GERD

- Aversion to food and general oral aversion
- Refusing to eat, or eating very little, even when hungry
- Anemia
- Runny nose
- Frequent sinus infections
- Excessive drooling
- Difficulty in swallowing, or gagging when eating
- Persistent sore throat or hoarse voice
- Apnea (stopping breathing for at least twenty seconds)
- Persistent ear infections
- Wheezing, asthma, and other respiratory problems
- Weight loss or failure to thrive
- Bad breath
- Arching of back or neck during or after meals
- Baby gagging himself with his fingers

Most children grow out of their infant reflux by the age of two. In fact, many parents notice an improvement when solid foods are introduced.

BIRTH TO SIX MONTHS

How Much Milk Should My Baby Be Having?

If you are breast-feeding, you won't know exactly how much milk baby is getting, unless they sometimes have an expressed feed. If he is thriving and the breasts are regularly emptied, then all is probably well. Your pediatrician or family doctor can give you any advice and reassurance you need. As a guide:

Baby's Age	Ounces per Feed
Newborns	1–2 oz
1 month old	3–4 oz
2–6 months old	4–6 oz
6 months	6–7½ oz
7 months +	Your baby needs between 16 and 27 oz every day until he is about a year old.
	The nutrients in the milk provide a safety net while you are gradually introducing solids.
	Since your baby's milk intake is reduced when he starts solids, you will need to provide more water. This must be boiled and then cooled for hygiene.

A Guide for a Good Daily Routine

We've all heard this pearl of wisdom: "babies thrive on routine." Not everyone is a routine person, but I found that the sooner I could establish the bones of a daily routine, the better for baby and all concerned (especially me).

Here is the routine my mum guided me through with my first and subsequent babies, literally from their birth. I have done easier things, but my oh my, how wonderful it was when they started living the routine.

Time	Activity
5:30 am (hopefully later)	Wakes and usually waits 30 minutes for a feed.
6:00	Milk feed. Some babies will fall straight back to sleep, others want a little play.
7:00	Look for tired signs and settle into sleep.
8:00–9:30	Length of sleep will vary but if he wakes early, encourage him to be resting and not tiring himself out before his next feed. This might be a good time to go for a walk.
9:30	Milk feed.

9:30	Play.
11:00–11:30	Look for tired signs and settle into sleep (around two hours after last waking time). If he wakes early keep him resting in a sling or swing until his next feed.
1:30 pm	Milk feed. Play.
3:00–3:30	Look for tired signs and settle into sleep (around two hours after last waking time).
5:00	Milk feed. Play. Bath. Top-up milk feed. Look for tired signs.
7:00–7:30	Settle for sleep.
Overnight	Offer baby a milk feed around 10:00 until solids are given and three meals a day are being eaten.

Believe me, this takes a little work, but it will be well worth it and *sooo* much easier for the beloved grandparents when babysitting on the rare (but much needed) nights that parents venture out together.

If your baby is beautiful and perfect, never cries or fusses,
sleeps on schedule, and burps on demand, an angel all the time...
you are the *grandma*!

God bless grandmas.

FOUR TO SIX MONTHS

When Is the Best Age to Start?

Most pediatricians recommend you wait until your baby is at least four to six months old before commencing solids, preferably closer to six.

This is vastly different from the days when I was a baby (1970) and the advice was rice cereal at six weeks...or else! Today there are a few very good reasons to wait to introduce solids to your beautiful baby:

- His digestive system is too immature for solid foods before four months. Although he can suck very well, he does not have a lot of saliva to help digest food.

- A young baby is not developmentally ready to eat solid foods. His throat muscles are not developed enough to swallow solid foods until he's at least four months old. And it is not until about four months that he's able to use his tongue to transfer food from the front to the back of his mouth.

- He needs a way to communicate that he has "had enough." If you're feeding him by breast or bottle, he will simply stop sucking or fall asleep, indicating that he's full. With solids his only means of letting you know he's full is to turn his head away, and he cannot do this until at least four or five months of age.

- Beginning solid foods too early has been associated with problems linked to intolerances and allergies.

Signs to Look For to Indicate Baby's Readiness

Weight   He weighs twice as much as his birth weight.

Sitting   He can sit with support, allowing him to lean forward when he wants another spoonful and backward to refuse.

Muscle Control He can control his head and neck muscles and turn his head to refuse food.

Breast-feeding He is breast-feeding at least eight to ten times per twenty-four hours; he empties both breasts at each feed and still wants more.

Drinking   He is drinking at least 16 to 25 ounces of formula per twenty-four hours and still wants more.

Feeding Time   The time between feeds becomes shorter and shorter over a period of several days.

Hand Movement   He can bring an object in his hand directly to his mouth.

Alertness   He shows interest in others eating around him and what they are eating.

Sleeping   His sleeps are becoming shorter instead of longer.

Rice Cereal

This is an appropriate meal to start your baby on. Offer one to two teaspoons mixed with breast milk or formula midway through a milk feed. If formula, choose a brand that is sugar-free and enriched with vitamins and iron and follow the instructions.

PUREES
Fruit Purees

Makes approximately 1 cup or 16 cubes (1 tablespoon per cube)

Try each individually before mixing to determine what your baby is receptive to.

Fruit	Quantity
Apple	14 oz (400g)
Apricot	12 oz (350g)
Avocado, 2 small	14 oz (400g)
Banana, 2 medium	14 oz (400g)
Cantaloupe	18 oz (500g)
Mango	14 oz (400g)
Peach	12 oz (350g)

- Peel, pit, seed, or core, and coarsely chop the individual fruit you wish to try.
- Mash the avocado and banana until smooth.
- Blend or process the other fruits until smooth.
- Offer your child as much fruit puree as desired.

Vegetable Purees

Makes approximately 1 cup or 16 cubes (1 tablespoon per cube)

Try each individually before mixing to determine what your baby is receptive to.

Vegetable	Weight	Cooking Time
Broccoli	9 oz (250g)	8 minutes
Carrot, 2 large	12 oz (360g)	15 minutes
Cauliflower	9 oz (250g)	8 minutes
Parsnip, 2 large	12 oz (360g)	12 minutes
Potato	14 oz (400g)	15 minutes
Spinach	9 oz (250g)	8 minutes
Sweet potato	14 oz (400g)	15 minutes
Winter squash	14 oz (400g)	15 minutes
Zucchini, 2 medium	10 oz (300g)	7 minutes

- Coarsely chop broccoli, cauliflower, and spinach.
- Peel, seed or core, and coarsely chop carrot, parsnip, potato, sweet potato, winter squash, and zucchini.
- Steam vegetables in 2 tablespoons water until tender; drain.
- Blend or process with a little liquid of choice (formula, breast milk, or the water used to cook the vegetable) until nice and smooth.
- Offer your child as much vegetable puree as desired.

When starting out, it was recommended to me that I start my baby on pureed vegetables first, before sweet fruits. This stands to reason, doesn't it—the sweetness of apples and pears over carrots and broccoli would be more likely to appeal to little palates. However, I found my boys to prefer fruits as their first baby foods and hence my menu planner reflects what worked for me. Fruit or veggies, it's all good stuff!

Once single foods have been introduced successfully, you can start to make mixed meals. Here are some handy basics. Good luck with these and with trying your own singles and combos, too.

For the purposes of this book, I have assumed your baby is six months old and have started the age count from then.

If your baby is younger, for example, four months old, when starting solids, just take off two months from the timeline.

Apple Cream

MAKES 1 CUP

1 apple
¼ cup water
2 tablespoons rice cereal
2 tablespoons breast milk or formula

- Peel, core, and coarsely chop the apple.
- Pop the apple into a saucepan with the water, bring to a boil, reduce the heat, and simmer uncovered for 10 minutes, or until tender.
- Blend or process until smooth and allow to cool.
- Mix the rice cereal and milk until creamy. Add the apple and mix before serving.

Apple Puree

MAKES ½ CUP

🔄 🚫 🐄 V ❄️

1 apple
¼ cup water

- Peel, core, and coarsely chop the apple.
- Pop the apple into a saucepan with the water, bring to a boil, reduce the heat, cover, and cook for 10 minutes. Stir occasionally to ensure the food doesn't stick to the bottom of the pan.
- Puree to serve.

 = Health is wealth!

Baby's Mashed Avocado

MAKES ½ CUP

¼ avocado, pitted and peeled

- Mash with a fork until a very soft and creamy consistency.

 = Protein power!

Carrot & Broccoli Puree

MAKES 1 CUP

1 medium carrot
½ cup water
4 broccoli florets
1 tablespoon breast milk or formula, to thin

- Peel and slice the carrot.
- Bring the water to a boil in a small saucepan, add the carrot, return to a boil, and cook for 3 minutes.
- Add the broccoli and continue to cook for 4 minutes, or until the veggies are tender.
- Drain, add the milk, and puree.

 +  = *Strong bones, teeth, and eyes!*

Carrot Soup

MAKES 1 CUP

2 small carrots, peeled and sliced
1 cup water
½ teaspoon chopped parsley

- Gently boil the carrots in the water in a small covered saucepan.
- Add the parsley. Puree to make a thick soup.

= High in vitamin A!

Pear Cream

MAKES 1 CUP

1 large pear
¼ cup water
2 tablespoons rice cereal
2 tablespoons breast milk or formula

- Peel, core, and coarsely chop the pear.
- Place in a small saucepan with the water.
- Bring to a boil, reduce the heat, and simmer uncovered for 15 to 20 minutes, or until tender.
- Blend or process until smooth. Allow to cool.
- Mix the rice cereal and milk until creamy. Add the pear and mix before serving.

Pear Puree

MAKES ½ CUP

1 pear
¼ cup water

- Peel, core, and coarsely chop the pear.
- Place the pear in a saucepan with the water, bring to a boil, reduce the heat, cover, and cook for 10 minutes.
- Stir occasionally to ensure the food doesn't stick to the bottom of the pan.
- Puree.

Love is a fruit in season at all times.
—Mother Teresa

Squash & Apple Puree

MAKES 1 CUP

7 ounces (200g) peeled, seeded, and chopped winter squash
¼ cup water
1 apple, peeled, cored, and coarsely chopped

- Place the squash in a saucepan and just cover with the water.
- Bring to a boil, reduce the heat, cover, and simmer for 10 minutes. Add the apple and continue to simmer until both are nice and tender.
- Drain, reserving a little of the liquid. Puree, using the liquid to achieve a smooth, runny consistency.

For a yummy combination, add some corn with the apple.

Squash Puree

MAKES 1 CUP

⓪ ⊗ ⓪ Ⓥ ✳

14 ounces (400g) winter squash, seeded, strings removed
1 cup water

- Preheat the oven to 350°F.
- Place the squash cut side down in a baking dish. Pour the water around it. Bake for 40 to 50 minutes.
- Scrape out the flesh, then puree.

 = *Glorious goodness!*

SEVEN MONTHS

Apple & Cinnamon Creamed Rice

MAKES 1 CUP

½ cup (40g) cooked rice
¼ cup breast milk or formula
½ green apple, peeled, cored, chopped, and cooked until soft
Pinch of ground cinnamon

- Combine all the ingredients in a saucepan. Cook very gently over low heat for 10 minutes, or until the rice is heated through.
- Check the temperature and mash to serve.

Apple & Pear Puree

MAKES 1 CUP

1 apple, peeled
1 pear, peeled
1 tablespoon water

- Cut the apple and pear into quarters, remove the cores, place in a bowl with the water, cover, and microwave for 4 minutes.
- Puree in a blender.

This fruit puree is convenient for dessert, for mixing with baby's cereal, or for adding to steamed chicken for an interesting dinner.

Apple, Parsnip & Squash Puree

MAKES 1 CUP

4 ounces (100g) parsnip
4 ounces (100g) seeded winter squash
1 green apple, peeled, cored, and chopped

- Wash, peel, and dice the parsnip and squash. Place in a medium saucepan and just cover with water. Bring to a gentle boil and cook for 10 minutes.
- Add the apple and cook for 5 minutes more, or until everything is tender.
- Drain, reserving any liquid. Puree until smooth, adding reserved liquid if necessary.

+ = *The bold and the beautiful!*

Apricot & Rutabaga Puree

MAKES 1 CUP

7 ounces (200g) rutabaga
2 fresh ripe apricots

- Wash, peel, and cube the rutabaga. Halve and pit the apricots.
- Steam the rutabaga for 15 to 20 minutes, or until tender. Add the apricots 5 minutes before the end of the cooking time.
- Puree in a blender until smooth, adding water if needed.

Avocado & Creamy Mashed Potato

MAKES 1½ CUPS

1 pound (450g) potatoes
2 cups water
2 avocados, pitted, peeled, and coarsely chopped

- Peel the potatoes and cut into large chunks. Cook in a large saucepan of boiling water for 8 minutes, or until tender.
- Drain the potatoes. Add the avocados and mash until nice and smooth.

+ = Lots of *fabulous fiber!*

Avocado-Mango Mousse

MAKES 1 CUP

½ cup peeled and cubed mango
½ cup chopped avocado flesh

- Mash the mango really well.
- Add the avocado and mash together. Whisk until a creamy mousse-like consistency forms.

Banana & Cherry Mousse

MAKES 1 CUP

6 sweet cherries, halved and pitted
1 tablespoon water
1 ripe banana, mashed
1 tablespoon rice cereal

- Pop the cherries into a small saucepan with the water and simmer for 2 to 3 minutes.
- Add the banana and simmer for 1 minute.
- Puree. Stir in the rice cereal for a thick, creamy, mousse-like consistency.

*This was my son Hamilton's first-ever Christmas lunch . . .
followed by Jell-O (keeping it real!).*

Banana & Pear Rice Cereal

MAKES 1 CUP

¼ pear, peeled, cored, and coarsely chopped
½ cup breast milk or formula
3 tablespoons rice cereal
½ banana

- Steam the pear for 5 to 6 minutes, until soft. Set aside.
- Meanwhile, warm the milk in a small saucepan.
- Mix the cereal into the warm milk to form a smooth consistency.
- Place the pear and banana in a small bowl and mash with a fork until smooth.
- Stir the fruits into the cereal and mix well.
- Serve immediately.

For a scrummy Banana & Squash "Smash," mix ½ cup squash puree and 1 ripe banana until combined.

Bananavo

MAKES ½ CUP

¼ banana
¼ avocado

- Mash together thoroughly.

You can also substitute ¼ cup cooked apple for the banana to make a lovely Appavo!

+ = Love at first bite!

Carrot & Parsnip Puree

MAKES ¾ CUP

1 carrot
1 parsnip
½ teaspoon butter

- Peel the carrot and parsnip and cut into pieces roughly the same size.
- Place into a small saucepan and cover with water. Boil for 20 minutes, or until tender.
- Drain and place in a blender. Add the butter and blend until smooth.

Chicken & Grape Puree

MAKES ¾ CUP

3 ounces (80g) skinless, boneless chicken breast, diced
2 tablespoons water
10 red seedless grapes

- Steam the chicken in a saucepan with the water until cooked through and soft.
- Cool, then pour into a blender. Add the grapes and puree.

I grew up on a farm and the first thing Dad planted was five acres of grapes. My family has always loved them on their own, in salads, with a cheese and baguette, and blended with other foods, as above. Happy memories!

Chicken, Rice & Veggies

MAKES 2 CUPS

1 cup water
1 skinless, boneless chicken breast half, cubed
¼ cup (45g) raw rice
2 carrots, peeled and thinly sliced
4 ounces (120g) green beans, trimmed but left whole

- Combine the water, chicken, and rice in a medium saucepan and simmer for 20 minutes.
- Add the carrots and beans. Simmer for 10 minutes.
- Drain, reserving any liquid. Place the chicken and vegetables in a blender and add enough reserved liquid to make a moist, smooth consistency.

Orchard Fruit Puree

MAKES 1½ CUPS

1 small Granny Smith apple
1 small pear
1 small peach
¼ cup water

- Wash, peel, and core the apple and pear, then chop into small pieces. Peel, pit, and chop the peach.
- Pop the fruits into a small saucepan, add the water, and gently boil for 5 minutes, or until soft.
- Drain, reserving the liquid, and puree until smooth, adding a little of the water from the saucepan if necessary.

I mentally willed my children to like this dish, because I loved the name so much: Orchard Fruit. Just thinking about it makes me feel healthier!

Peachy Chicken

MAKES 1 CUP

⅓ cup (30g) chopped cooked chicken
¼ cup (40g) cooked rice
1 very ripe peach, peeled, pitted, and coarsely chopped
1 tablespoon breast milk or formula (optional)

- Mix the chicken, rice, and peach together.
- Puree to desired consistency, adding milk if desired.

*You may add veggies or fruits to any of the meat recipes.
Adding fruits to meat helps to sweeten if at first
your baby doesn't seem too fond of meat.*

Power Puree

MAKES 2 CUPS

½ cup peeled, seeded, and diced winter squash
1 cup water
1 apple, peeled, cored, and diced
1 ripe banana

- Place the squash in a saucepan, cover with the water, and simmer for 5 minutes.
- Add the apple and simmer for 5 minutes more, or until both are soft.
- Cool the squash and apple mixture for 10 minutes.
- Transfer to a blender and puree until smooth.
- Mash the banana and mix it into the puree.
- Serve warm.

 +  = *Treasure trove of nutrients!*

Sweet Potato with Asian Pear

MAKES 1 CUP

½ cup (80g) cooked rice
2 cups water
½ cup (100g) peeled and cubed sweet potato
½ Asian pear

- Place the rice in a saucepan and cover with the water.
- Add the sweet potato.
- Bring to a boil, then lower the heat and simmer for 25 minutes, or until everything is soft.
- Wash, peel, core, and chop the pear. Place it in a steamer and steam over boiling water until soft.
- Mash the pear and sweet potato mixture together.

Tropicana Pudding

MAKES ½ CUP

⅓ cup water
2 teaspoons farina
½ banana, mashed
¼ mango, peeled and mashed

- Put the water and farina in a small saucepan over low heat and whisk until thick.
- Remove from the heat and stir in the banana and mango.

All three of my sons looooved this delightful dessert.

= Healthy he♥rt!

Veggielicious

MAKES 2 CUPS

1 cup peeled and diced winter squash
1 cup broccoli florets
1 carrot, peeled and diced

- Steam all the vegetables until tender.
- Mash or blend.

Add a little fresh corn, cut from the cob, when steaming, for natural sweetness.

 +  +  = Nutrient rich!

EIGHT TO TEN MONTHS

Apple & Apricot Crumble

MAKES 1 CUP

1 cup fresh fine white bread crumbs
¼ cup heavy cream
1 teaspoon lemon juice
2 tablespoons peeled and diced apple
2 tablespoons diced dried apricot

- Pop all the ingredients into a bowl.
- Using a stick blender, blend and serve.

I still make this for Flynn, and he is now three.
My babies have all enjoyed it; I hope yours do, too!

Banana Maple Cream

MAKES ¾ CUP

½ cup (125g) Greek-style yogurt
1 teaspoon maple syrup
½ banana, mashed

- Mix all the ingredients together in a small bowl and serve—yummy!

*A great use for the leftover banana is to blend it with
2 ounces (50g) of silken tofu for a delicious "Banana Mousse."*

= Very versatile!

Breakfast Polenta

MAKES 2 CUPS

1 cup cornmeal
4 cups water
2 cups milk
¼ cup brown sugar
1 teaspoon vanilla extract
½ teaspoon ground cinnamon
½ teaspoon grated nutmeg

- In a small bowl, mix the cornmeal with 1 cup of water.
- In a medium saucepan, bring the milk and 3 cups of water to a boil. Reduce the heat to low and slowly add the cornmeal, whisking constantly. Simmer for 10 minutes, or until the mixture thickens; continue whisking to remove any lumps.
- Add the sugar, vanilla, cinnamon, and nutmeg, and stir to combine. Serve warm.

Carrot, Lentil & Coriander Puree

MAKES 2 CUPS

1 potato
2 carrots
3 tablespoons (50g) red lentils (rinse under water, discarding debris)
½ teaspoon ground coriander
1¼ cups breast milk or formula
Boiling water (optional)

- Peel and dice the potato and carrots and place in a saucepan with the lentils and coriander. Add the milk and bring to a boil.
- Cover and simmer for approximately 40 minutes, or until the lentils are very soft.
- Top up with boiling water if necessary.
- Cool a little, then puree until smooth.

Adding a sprinkle of herbs or a dash of spice can turn a plain and uninspiring dish into something exciting that your baby may really enjoy. Just remember to treat herbs, spices, and garlic as you would any new food; introduce them from six months of age, separately, to see how baby likes them.

Cheesy Cauliflower, Leek & Tater Mix

MAKES 1 CUP

1 teaspoon unsalted butter
1 ounce (25g) leek, white part only, thinly sliced and washed well
5 ounces (150g) peeled and diced sweet potato
1 cup boiling water
2½ ounces (75g) cauliflower, cut into florets
2 ounces (30g) grated cheddar cheese (about ½ cup)

- Melt the butter in a frying pan and add the leek. Sauté gently for 3 minutes, or until soft.
- Add the sweet potato and water and cook for 5 minutes.
- Add the cauliflower, cover, and cook for 10 minutes, or until tender.
- Pour the mixture into a blender, add the grated cheese, and whiz together.
- Serve warm.

 = Eat me, I'm yummy!

Chicken & Apple Sticks

MAKES 8 STICKS

1 medium apple
1 medium carrot
½ clove garlic
½ small onion
9 ounces (250g) ground chicken
1 egg yolk, beaten
¼ cup (15g) fresh bread crumbs
Pinch of crushed dried thyme
Pinch of ground black pepper

- Preheat the broiler. Line a broiler pan with aluminum foil.
- Peel the apple, carrot, garlic, and onion and grate into a mixing bowl.
- Add the chicken, egg yolk, bread crumbs, thyme, and pepper and mix well.
- Take small balls of the mixture and roll into 8 little sticks.
- Place on the broiler pan and broil for 8 minutes on each side, turning once.
- Allow to cool before serving, to the glee of your baby!

Chicken & Vegetable Casserole

MAKES 2 CUPS

1 tablespoon olive oil
1 carrot, peeled and grated
½ stalk celery, diced
½ leek, white part only, sliced and washed well
1 clove garlic, roasted
2 potatoes, peeled and diced
4 ounces (120g) diced chicken thigh meat
1 cup chicken stock
1 cup water

- Heat the oil in a saucepan over medium heat. Sauté the carrot, celery, leek, and garlic for 6 to 7 minutes, or until soft.
- Add the potatoes, chicken, and stock. Add water until the liquid barely covers the contents. Cover and boil gently for 20 minutes, or until the potatoes are soft and the chicken is cooked.
- Use a stick blender to blend to a smooth consistency.
- As your baby grows and can eat chunkier consistencies, blend accordingly.

This meal is both delicious and nutritious and it makes you feel like Mother of the Year because you know the goodness your baby's little body is getting.

Fruity Pudding

MAKES 4 PORTIONS

1 pear, peeled, cored, and chopped
2 fresh apricots, pitted and chopped
1 tablespoon orange juice
1 tablespoon water
1 tablespoon custard powder or vanilla pudding mix
½ cup breast milk or formula

- Place the pear and apricots in a small saucepan with the orange juice and water. Bring to a boil, reduce the heat, cover, and simmer for 10 minutes, or until the fruit is soft. Gently mash with a fork.
- Meanwhile, blend the custard powder with 2 tablespoons of the milk.
- Mix in the remaining milk, transfer to a saucepan, and heat, stirring until thick and smooth.
- Add the fruit puree and mix to combine.

You can substitute nectarines, apples, or seedless berries for the apricots. Look for lovely, sweet fruits in season, as they are delicious without added sugar.

Gobble Gobble Stew

(or "Obble Obble," as my boys called it!)

MAKES 6 PORTIONS

1 potato
1 carrot
4 ounces (115g) turkey breast (skin removed)
Kernels cut from ½ ear corn
1¼ cups breast milk or formula

- Peel the potato and carrot, rinse, and cut into small cubes. Cut the turkey into thin strips. Place the potato, carrot, and turkey in a small saucepan. Add the corn and milk. Cover and simmer for 20 minutes, until the turkey is cooked thoroughly.
- Puree until completely smooth.

Oo La La Toast

MAKES 2 PORTIONS

1 egg yolk
1 tablespoon milk
½ teaspoon ground cinnamon
2 slices day-old sandwich bread
1 tablespoon (15g) butter

- Place the egg yolk in a shallow bowl and beat in the milk and cinnamon until well blended.
- Remove the crusts from the bread and cut each slice into three fingers.
- Melt the butter in a frying pan. Working in batches, dip each finger into the egg mix, making sure both sides are well coated. Place in the pan and cook on both sides until golden brown.
- Repeat with the remaining fingers, adding more butter if needed.

Serve drizzled with pure maple syrup.
Pure maple syrup is more expensive but a much healthier option.
I always look for it on special!

Squash & Tater Cheese Pie

MAKES 8 PORTIONS

Olive oil spray
2 large potatoes
1 pound (500g) seeded winter squash
2 slices bacon
1½ cups (150g) grated cheddar cheese

- Preheat the oven to 350°F. Spray a baking dish with olive oil.
- Peel the potatoes and squash and chop into roughly the same size chunks.
- Pop both into a saucepan of boiling water, reduce the heat so that the water continues to bubble but not boil over, and cook for 15 minutes, or until the vegetables are tender.
- Meanwhile, cut the bacon into small pieces and lightly fry.
- Drain and mash the potatoes and squash. Stir in 1 cup of the cheese.
- Spoon into the baking dish. Sprinkle with the bacon and the remaining cheese. Bake until the cheese has melted and is nice and golden.

 + = The perfect pair!

Vegetable Medley

MAKES 2 CUPS

¼ cup water

1 sweet potato, peeled and chopped

1 carrot, peeled and chopped

3 tablespoons corn kernels

1 zucchini, chopped

1 tablespoon peas

- Bring the water to a boil in a small saucepan. Add the sweet potato, carrot, and corn to the water, cover, and simmer for approximately 8 minutes.
- Add the zucchini and peas and continue cooking for 4 minutes, or until all the veggies are tender.
- Drain and blend until nice and creamy.

This dish fulfills baby's daily veggie quota.

Baby Finger Foods — Handy Hints and Tips

As with most things "baby," there are no hard-and-fast rules. But finger foods can generally be introduced at around seven to eight months of age, when your baby is sitting up unassisted and hand-eye coordination has developed.

At this stage the concern is to prevent choking. Babies do not have the back teeth needed to chew and grind lumps of food properly. Food swallowed in largish pieces is more likely to get stuck in the throat and cut off the airway. So always supervise what your little angel pops into his mouth and *never* leave him to feed himself alone.

To encourage chewing, food should progress from puree, to mash, to small lumps, and then to largish lumps.

When your baby starts to pick things up with his hands, at around eight to ten months, try introducing "finger foods" such as:

- Cheese sticks, sliced from a block of cheese
- Thin strips of chicken, meat, or ham
- Bread and dry toast rusks or zwieback
- Cooked pasta
- Pieces of well-cooked fruits and vegetables such as apple, pear, potato, carrot, and squash
- Pieces of soft raw fruit such as banana, mango, and peach

Some tips to make life easier:

- Introduce finger foods one at a time and slowly add new ones. Offer a variety of colors and textures.
- Your baby will want to touch, smell, taste, and play with his food. Stay relaxed about the mess and let him experiment.
- To keep mess to a minimum, only give your baby two or three pieces of food at a time—any more will probably end up on the floor!
- Put the food in a suction-type bowl that will stick to the table, or straight onto the high-chair table itself.
- Coat slippery foods, like banana or avocado, in powdered cereal or finely crushed wheat germ—it makes them easier to pick up.
- If your baby doesn't like a certain type of food, try it again a few weeks later; babies' tastes change all the time. If he refuses all finger foods, be patient and keep trying. You're sure to offer him something that will catch his interest eventually.
- Baby finger foods make perfect snacks between meals to "tide your baby over." But be careful not to allow your baby more snacks than he really needs, as he may become less interested at mealtimes.
- If your baby is teething, offer him cold finger foods to soothe his gums— try freezing pieces of melon or banana for the ultimate in gum relief!
- Pack some healthy travel snacks for baby whenever you hop in the car. There are pros and cons about doing this but, personally, I found it very helpful because it kept my boys occupied while traveling from point A to point B.

TEN TO TWELVE MONTHS

Beef Casserole

MAKES 4 PORTIONS

1 tablespoon olive oil
1 small onion, peeled and finely chopped
1 clove garlic, peeled and crushed
4 ounces (120g) cubed stewing meat, trimmed of fat (such as beef chuck)
1 carrot, peeled and sliced
1 potato, peeled and diced
1 tablespoon golden raisins
2/3 cup tomato-based pasta sauce
3/4 cup chicken stock

- Heat the oil in a small saucepan and sauté the onion gently for 4 to 5 minutes.
- Add the garlic and meat and sauté, stirring, until browned.
- Add the carrot, potato, and raisins. Pour in the tomato puree and stock. Bring to a boil, stir, cover, and simmer gently for about 1 hour, or until the meat is tender, adding more stock or water if necessary, and stirring occasionally.
- Leave to cool slightly, then puree in a food processor or blender.

Cooking beef slowly with veggies and dried fruit makes it tender and appealing to babies (and their parents).

Chicken Sticks

MAKES 4 STICKS

1 cup cornflakes
2 tablespoons grated Parmesan cheese
2 chicken tenderloins, halved lengthwise
2 tablespoons Greek-style yogurt

- Preheat the oven to 350°F. Line a baking sheet with parchment paper.
- Crush the cornflakes finely and mix thoroughly with the Parmesan cheese.
- Roll the chicken first in yogurt, then in the cornflake mix.
- Place the pieces on the baking sheet and bake for 8 to 10 minutes, or until the chicken is cooked through and golden.
- Serve warm.

Green & Gold Nuggets

MAKES 20 NUGGETS

20 bite-size broccoli florets
2 egg yolks, beaten
1 slice whole wheat bread, grated to fine crumbs
½ cup (50g) grated cheddar cheese

- Preheat the oven to 350°F. Line a baking sheet with parchment paper.
- Dip the broccoli in the egg yolks, coating well.
- Mix together the bread crumbs and cheese on a plate. Coat the broccoli in the mixture.
- Place on the baking sheet and bake for 15 to 18 minutes, flipping halfway.
- Serve soft and warm.

 = *Our healthy hero!*

Impossible Pie

MAKES ONE 10-INCH PIE (12 PORTIONS)

A recipe from Marie McColl, loving mother to four and grandmother to eight.

4 eggs, lightly beaten
2 cups milk
1 cup (200g) superfine sugar
½ cup (85g) all-purpose flour
1 cup (120g) unsweetened flaked coconut
½ cup (115g) butter
2 tablespoons vanilla extract
Stewed fruit, for serving

- Preheat the oven to 350°F. Line a 10-inch pie plate with a circle of parchment paper.
- Place all the ingredients (except the stewed fruit) in a large bowl and mix thoroughly. Pour into the pie plate.
- Bake for 1 hour, or until the center is firm.
- Cool before cutting. Serve with some stewed fruit.

*Serve this yummy pie closer to twelve months
due to the inclusion of the entire egg.*

Lentil & Sweet Potato Puree

MAKES 4 PORTIONS

1 small onion, peeled and finely chopped
½ red bell pepper, seeded and chopped
1 tablespoon water
1 tomato, cut into chunks
3 tablespoons (50g) red lentils, rinsed
3 ounces (150g) sweet potato, peeled and chopped
1 cup vegetable stock

- Cook the onion and bell pepper in the water in a nonstick frying pan for 4 minutes.
- Add the tomato and continue cooking for 1 minute.
- Add the lentils, sweet potato, and stock and bring to a boil. Reduce the heat and simmer for 20 to 25 minutes, or until the lentils are quite mushy.
- Cool for 10 minutes before pureeing.

Melon Balls

¼ honeydew melon, seeded
¼ cantaloupe, seeded
⅛ seedless watermelon
1 tablespoon orange juice

- Use a melon baller to scoop out balls from each of the fruits. You should have about 1 cup of each.
- Drizzle with orange juice and serve for a fresh, fun, and colorful snack.

Mini Patty Cakes

MAKES 24 CUPCAKES

2 tablespoons (30g) butter
3 tablespoons superfine sugar
2 drops vanilla extract
1 egg
1 cup (175g) self-rising flour
2 tablespoons breast milk or formula
Icing (optional)

- Preheat the oven to 350°F. Line two 12-cup mini muffin pans with paper cups.
- With an electric mixer, cream together the butter and sugar until light and fluffy. Add the vanilla and egg and continue beating until well combined.
- Add the flour alternately with a drizzle of milk, mixing thoroughly.
- Spoon the mixture into the cups. Bake for 20 minutes, or until done.
- Cool in the pan. Lovely served plain or iced.

To test if any cake is done, take a skewer and insert it into the center of the cake. If it comes out clean, the cake is cooked through.

Minestrone Soup

MAKES 8 PORTIONS

2 tablespoons (30g) butter
1 slice bacon
1 large potato, peeled and diced
2 stalks celery, chopped
1 small leek, quartered lengthwise, thinly sliced, and washed well
1 carrot, peeled and diced
7 cups chicken stock
2 tablespoons tomato paste
¼ cup broken spaghetti
2 cups thinly sliced napa cabbage
¼ cup peas
1 clove garlic, peeled and crushed

- In a large, heavy saucepan, melt the butter. Lightly cook the bacon, potato, celery, leek, and carrot until soft.
- Add the stock and bring to a boil.
- Reduce the heat and simmer for 20 minutes.
- Add the tomato paste, spaghetti, cabbage, peas, and garlic and continue to simmer until the spaghetti is tender.

This is so yummy, I always have it in my freezer!

No-Stir Squash Risotto

MAKES 4 PORTIONS

4 tablespoons (60g) butter
½ small onion, peeled and finely diced
3 slices bacon, finely diced
8 ounces (200g) mushrooms, cleaned and finely chopped
2 cups (370g) Arborio rice
5 cups chicken stock
1½ pounds (700g) peeled, seeded, and diced winter squash
½ cup (50g) grated Parmesan cheese

- Preheat the oven to 375°F.
- Melt the butter and fry the onion, bacon, and mushrooms until the bacon is crisp.
- Pop all ingredients into a casserole dish and mix well.
- Cook, uncovered, for 40 minutes.
- Stir and serve.

 =

Loaded with the antioxidant beta-carotene!

Orzo with Spring Herb Pesto

MAKES 4 PORTIONS

4 cups arugula
4 cups basil leaves
1 cup (160g) pine nuts, toasted
½ cup (50g) grated Parmesan cheese, plus more for garnish
1 tablespoon crushed garlic
1¼ cups extra virgin olive oil
Pinch of ground pepper
1½ cups orzo

- In a food processor, combine the arugula, basil, pine nuts, Parmesan, and garlic.
- With the motor running, add 1 cup of the olive oil in a slow stream until emulsified.
- Add the pepper. Set aside.
- Bring a large pot of water to a boil. Add the orzo and cook according to package directions until very soft. Drain well, reserving ¼ cup of the pasta water.
- In a large bowl, combine the pesto with the remaining ¼ cup olive oil and half the reserved pasta water (add more if needed). The pesto should acquire a sauce-like consistency. Add the orzo and toss to combine.
- Serve garnished with extra cheese.

Peach Delights

MAKES 12 PIECES

½ banana
2 tablespoons plain yogurt
½ peach, pitted
2 tablespoons rolled oats, blended to powder in a food processor

- Mash the banana together with the yogurt until well blended.
- Peel the peach half and cut into 12 cubes. Roll in the yogurt-and-banana mixture, coating well.
- Roll the peach cubes in the oats to make them easy for your baby to pick up and enjoy!

Poached Salmon
with Garden Vegetables

MAKES 4 PORTIONS

²/₃ cup vegetable stock
1 potato, peeled and diced
1 carrot, peeled and diced
4 ounces (120g) salmon fillet, skinned and chopped
2 tablespoons peas
¹/₃ cup (30g) grated cheddar cheese

- Place the stock in a saucepan with the potato and carrot. Bring to a boil, then cook over medium heat for 7 to 8 minutes, or until the vegetables are just tender.
- Add the salmon and peas, cover, and simmer for 3 minutes, or until the fish flakes easily and the vegetables are very tender.
- Remove from the heat and stir in the cheese. Mash with a fork.
- Cool before serving.

To freeze, simply divide into 4 portions. Thaw overnight in the fridge, then reheat. Stir really well to distribute an even heat.

Pork & Apple Bake

6 ounces (175g) pork tenderloin or boneless loin chop
1 potato
1 parsnip
¼ onion
1 Granny Smith apple
1 cup water
2 fresh sage leaves

- Preheat the oven to 350°F.
- Rinse the pork and chop into small pieces. Peel and chop the potato, parsnip, and onion. Peel, quarter, core, and chop the apple. Place in a casserole with the water and sage.
- Cover and bake for 1 ¼ hours, or until nice and tender.
- Blend or mash to the required consistency.

The flavor of the apple brings out the best of the meat.

Sausage Rolls

MAKES 16 ROLLS

1 pound (500g) bulk sausage
1 carrot, peeled and grated
½ zucchini, grated
¼ onion, finely diced
3 tablespoons ketchup
½ teaspoon chopped fresh parsley
2 sheets frozen puff pastry (one 17.3-ounce/450g package), thawed in
the refrigerator

- Mix the sausage, carrot, and zucchini. Add the onion, ketchup, and parsley and mix well.
- Cut the pastry sheets in half lengthwise. Divide the sausage mixture into four and place along one long side of the pastry. Roll the pastry up over the filling, finishing with the seam of the pastry on the bottom. Return to the fridge for approximately 30 minutes to firm the pastry.
- While the rolls are chilling, preheat the oven to 350°F and line a rimmed baking sheet with parchment paper.
- With a sharp knife, cut each roll into eight pieces. Place on the baking sheet seam side down, and bake for 20 to 25 minutes, or until golden and crisp. Cool before serving.

Vegetable Rolls

MAKES 16

1 garlic clove, peeled and crushed
1 carrot, grated
1 zucchini, grated
Kernels cut from 1 ear of corn
½ cup cottage cheese
1½ cups quick-cooking rolled oats
½ teaspoon dried mixed herbs
1 egg, lightly beaten
2 sheets frozen puff pastry (one 17.3-ounce/450g package),
 thawed in the refrigerator

- Preheat the oven to 400°F. Line two baking sheets with parchment paper.
- In a large nonstick frying pan over medium heat, add the garlic, carrot, zucchini, and corn and cook, stirring occasionally, for 5 minutes or until the vegetables are just tender. Transfer the mixture to a bowl.
- Add the cottage cheese, oats, mixed herbs, and half the egg; stir to combine.
- Cut each pastry sheet in half or into strips approximately 3 inches wide. Evenly spoon the vegetable mixture along each long side of the pastry. Brush the opposite edges with egg. Roll up the pastry to enclose the filling. Cut the rolls into thirds and place onto the prepared sheets. Brush the tops of the rolls with the remaining egg.
- Bake for 15 to 20 minutes, or until puffed and golden.

A wise nurse once advised me:
Beware of imposing your standards on their taste.
If they want to eat banana smeared with ketchup—let them!

Baked Custard

MAKES 1 PORTION

½ cup milk
1 egg yolk
1 tablespoon superfine sugar
1 teaspoon butter
Pinch of grated nutmeg

- Preheat the oven to 350°F.
- In a small saucepan, heat the milk until warm.
- Lightly whisk together the egg and sugar.
- Stir the warm milk into the egg mixture.
- Grease a 6-ounce ramekin with the butter. Pour the custard into it. Sprinkle with the nutmeg.
- Bake in a water bath for 1 hour, or until firm; a knife blade inserted halfway between the edge and the center should come out clean.

A water bath is an ovenproof dish containing water into which the ramekin is placed. This prevents the custard from cooking too quickly and curdling.

Banana Pancakes

MAKES 8 PANCAKES

Fabalish!

1 egg
1 cup milk
1 cup (175g) self-rising flour
½ teaspoon ground cinnamon
1 ripe banana, mashed
1 tablespoon (15g) butter

- Beat the egg in a medium bowl. Whisk in the milk, flour, and cinnamon to form a thick paste.
- Fold in the mashed banana.
- Melt the butter in a nonstick frying pan. Dollop the batter into the pan and cook over medium heat for 2 to 3 minutes.
- When bubbles appear, flip and cook the other side for 2 minutes more, or until a light golden color.
- Repeat with the remaining batter.

Banana Fritters: For a variation of the above, mix the egg, milk, flour, and cinnamon together. Slice the banana and coat with the batter. Lightly fry in butter until golden brown. Serve as finger food or at breakfast time.

Coconut Pancakes

MAKES 12 PANCAKES

1 cup coconut milk
2 cups (350g) self-rising flour
2 tablespoons sugar
2 eggs, lightly beaten
½ cup water
2 tablespoons (30g) butter

- Combine the coconut milk, flour, sugar, eggs, and water in a large bowl and gently whisk until smooth.
- Melt half the butter in a nonstick frying pan, swirling to coat the entire surface.
- Pour in small dollops of batter and cook over medium heat until bubbles appear.
- Flip and cook until lightly browned. When done, transfer to a plate and cover with foil to keep warm.
- Repeat until all the batter is used, using more butter when required.

Leftover coconut milk can be frozen. Freeze it in an ice cube tray, then pop the cubes out and transfer to a resealable plastic bag until you need them.

Fruit Shakes

1 banana
3 tablespoons fruit juice
½ cup mixed frozen berries

- In a blender, whip together the banana, fruit juice, and berries for a nutritious shake.
- It's yummy—just remember to share it with your baby!

You can add 2 tablespoons of yogurt for more protein and calcium. For the consistency of a smoothie, use a frozen banana or add frozen yogurt.

Country Pork & Green Beans

MAKES 4 PORTIONS

4 ounces (120g) lean pork tenderloin

1 potato

1 carrot

1¼ cups water

3 fresh sage leaves

3 ounces (75g) green beans, trimmed and chopped into thirds

- Rinse the pork and chop into small pieces. Wash and peel the potato and carrot, then chop. Place the pork, potato, and carrot in a saucepan with the water and sage and bring to a boil.
- Reduce the heat, cover, and cook for 6 minutes.
- Add the beans and cook for 5 minutes, or until everything is cooked thoroughly.
- Mash or process.

Easy-Peasy Meatloaf

MAKES 8 PORTIONS

1 pound (500g) lean ground beef
3 eggs
2 pieces whole wheat bread, grated to fine crumbs
1 small zucchini, finely grated
¼ cup (70g) barbecue sauce

- Preheat the oven to 350°F. Line a 9 by 5-inch loaf pan with parchment paper.
- Thoroughly mix together the meat, eggs, bread crumbs, zucchini, and 3 tablespoons of the barbecue sauce and scrape into the loaf pan.
- Spread the reserved sauce on top.
- Bake for 50 minutes, or until browned on top.
- Slice into thin strips to serve.

*My boys love this served with a little mashed potato and some peas!
I sometimes make it with ground chicken and use
a lovely fruit chutney instead of barbecue sauce.*

Fried Rice

MAKES 4 PORTIONS

1 tablespoon (15g) butter
2 slices bacon, chopped
½ onion, finely diced
1½ cups frozen peas and corn, thawed
2 eggs, lightly beaten
2 cups (320g) cold cooked rice
1 tablespoon kecap manis or soy sauce

- In a large nonstick frying pan, melt the butter over medium heat. Add the bacon and onion and cook until the bacon is crispy.
- Add the peas and corn and cook for 2 minutes.
- Move the contents to the side of the pan and pour in the eggs, leaving them until cooked through.
- Break up the eggs. Add the rice and mix everything together. Stir until the rice is heated through.
- Serve with a drizzle of kecap manis.

*Kecap manis is a pantry staple in my house because
it has a more syrupy, sweeter flavor than normal soy sauce.
It is available in the Asian section of most supermarkets.*

Lamb in Lentils

MAKES 4 PORTIONS

4 ounces (120g) boneless lamb, trimmed of excess fat
4 ounces (120g) rutabaga
1 stalk celery
2 tablespoons (30g) red lentils, rinsed under cold water
1 tablespoon ketchup
1½ cups water

- Rinse the lamb and chop into small pieces. Peel and chop the rutabaga and chop the celery. Place all the ingredients in a saucepan and bring to a boil.
- Reduce the heat, cover, and simmer for 40 minutes, or until the lentils are tender. Top-up with a little extra water if it dries out.
- Mash together to a suitable texture.

Mini Meatballs in Tomato Sauce

MAKES 36 MEATBALLS

1 pound (500g) lean ground beef
1 teaspoon tomato paste
1 tablespoon chopped basil
1 slice whole wheat bread, grated into fine crumbs
1 egg
1 small onion, finely chopped
2 tablespoons olive oil
One 10.75-ounce (400g) can condensed tomato soup

- Mix the beef, tomato paste, basil, bread crumbs, egg, and onion in a large bowl. With clean, wet hands, roll into little balls about 1 inch (3 cm) across.
- Heat the olive oil in a frying pan over medium heat. Add the meatballs and cook for 5 minutes, rolling to seal the outside.
- Add the tomato soup and cook for 10 to 15 minutes more, or until the sauce is warm and thickens slightly.
- Serve with mashed potatoes and veggies.

My boys love these still!

Ocean Dinner

10 ounces (275g) sweet potato
1 small zucchini
4 ounces (120g) white fish fillet, such as tilapia
¾ cup milk

- Peel the sweet potato and slice thin. Dice the zucchini. Place the vegetables in a saucepan and top with the fish.
- Pour the milk over, bring to a boil, reduce the heat, cover, and simmer for 15 minutes, or until cooked through.
- Remove the fish and break it into pieces. Mash the fish together with the vegetables.

Peanut Butter Bread

MAKES ONE 9-INCH LOAF

1¼ cups milk
½ cup (130g) creamy peanut butter
⅓ cup (100g) Lyle's golden syrup or honey
2 tablespoons vegetable oil
1 teaspoon vanilla extract
2 cups (350g) self-rising flour, sifted

- Preheat the oven to 350°F. Line a 9 by 5-inch loaf pan with parchment paper.
- In a medium saucepan, bring the milk to a boil. Remove from the heat and beat in the peanut butter, golden syrup, oil, and vanilla until the mixture is smooth. Gradually add the milk mixture to the sifted flour, beating well after each addition. Pour into the prepared pan.
- Bake for 50 to 60 minutes.
- Cool before slicing to serve plain or with jam.
- Store in an airtight container.

Saucy Ham Pasta

MAKES 4 PORTIONS

¾ cup (50g) dried pasta shapes, such as small shells or wheels
⅓ cup (50g) frozen mixed vegetables
2 tablespoons (30g) butter
2 tablespoons all-purpose flour
½ cup milk (may need a little more)
½ cup (50g) grated cheddar cheese
2 slices ham, chopped

- Cook the pasta in a saucepan of boiling water for 5 minutes.
- Add the vegetables and cook for 5 minutes more, or until the pasta is al dente. Drain and set aside.
- Melt the butter in a saucepan and stir in the flour. Gradually add the milk and bring to a boil, stirring until the sauce thickens.
- Stir two-thirds of the grated cheese into the sauce. Add the pasta, veggies, and ham.
- Spoon into a shallow serving dish and sprinkle with the remaining cheese.

Shepherd's Pie

MAKES 4 PORTIONS

2 tomatoes
¼ onion
1 potato, peeled
2 ounces (50g) mushrooms, wiped clean
4 ounces (120g) lean ground beef
1 cup water
2 tablespoons ketchup
½ teaspoon chopped parsley

- Cut the tomatoes into quarters and remove the seeds. Finely chop the onion and potato. Slice the mushrooms.
- Brown the beef in a saucepan, breaking up any clumps with a spoon.
- Add the vegetables and cook for 5 minutes.
- Add the water, ketchup, and parsley and bring to a boil. Reduce the heat, cover, and simmer for 40 minutes, or until the potatoes are tender and the mixture thickens slightly.
- Mash lightly before serving.

Another one that's still a family favorite—it's delish!

Spring Vegetable Risotto

MAKES 4 PORTIONS

½ cup (90g) short-grain rice
1¼ cups milk
3 ounces (80g) finely chopped red bell pepper
1 small zucchini, finely chopped
½ stalk celery, finely chopped

- Place the rice and milk in a saucepan, bring to a boil, then simmer uncovered for 5 minutes.
- Add the red pepper, zucchini, and celery to the rice mixture.
- Bring to a boil again, reduce the heat, cover, and simmer for approximately 10 minutes, or until the rice is nice and soft.
- Mash lightly if needed.

Tuna, Corn & Rice Cakes

MAKES 12 CAKES

One 6-ounce (185g) can tuna in spring water, drained
½ cup (125g) cream-style corn (half of an 8.75-ounce/240g can)
⅓ cup (55g) cooked rice
1 tablespoon finely chopped red bell pepper
1 scallion (green onion), thinly sliced
1 tablespoon grated cheddar cheese
¼ cup (45g) self-rising flour
1 teaspoon dried mixed herbs, such as Italian seasoning
1 egg, lightly beaten
Olive oil spray

- Place all the ingredients (except the olive oil spray) in a medium bowl and mix well to combine.
- Lightly spray a nonstick frying pan. Place over medium heat. Dollop spoonfuls of the mixture into the hot pan. Cook for 2 to 3 minutes on each side, or until golden.
- Remove to absorbent paper to drain before serving with strips of steamed veggies.

As my mum says: eat more fish!

Yogurt Jell-O & Fruit Salad

◎

One 3-ounce (85g) package raspberry Jell-O
2 cups boiling water
2 tablespoons peach yogurt
2 slices honeydew melon, peeled and cubed
1 peach, peeled, pitted, and cubed

- Make the Jell-O as instructed on the package, using the boiling water.
- Whisk in the yogurt and allow to cool.
- Pour into a square baking dish and let set in the fridge.
- Cut into cubes and arrange in a bowl with the melon and peach.

IN THE CAR

Now, I've heard the debates, too: do you offer food in the car or do you not?

Ultimately it is up to you, but personally I found no more stressful a situation than being in the car with a screaming baby! As my babies became toddlers, I found life easier if I had some sort of healthy snack tucked away. Here are a few of my saviors for in the car and on the move. See the section on finger foods on page 78 for more ideas for portable food.

 = *Saviors!*

Carrot Chips

1 carrot
½ tablespoon butter, melted
1 tablespoon honey

- Preheat the oven to 350°F. Line a baking sheet with parchment paper.
- Peel and slice the carrot into ¼-inch (5mm) rounds.
- Lay the slices on the baking sheet in a single layer without overlapping.
- Mix together the butter and honey and drizzle over the carrot slices.
- Bake for 5 minutes, flip, and bake for another 5 to 8 minutes, or until the edges are golden.
- Cool before placing in a resealable plastic bag.

Cheese Sticks

1 slice cheese
1 slice sandwich bread, crusts removed

- Lay the slice of cheese on the bread.
- Broil until melted.
- Cool before cutting into 3 or 4 sticks.

Frozen Grapes

12 red seedless grapes

- Pop the grapes into a resealable plastic bag and freeze for at least 1½ hours.
- These keep for a very long time and you can make the recipe bigger or smaller.

Melon Cubes

8 ounces (200g) cantaloupe

- Peel, seed, and dice into small cubes about ½ inch in size.
- Place the cubes into a sealable container and chill until required.

Parmesan Pasta Spirals

½ cup cooked pasta spirals (rotelle or rotini)
1 tablespoon finely grated Parmesan cheese

- Place the pasta in a sealable container.
- Sprinkle with the Parmesan.
- Refrigerate until needed.

Parmesan, Pear & Raisins

½ ounce (10g) Parmesan, cheese, shaved into thin strips
¼ pear, peeled, cored, and sliced thin
10 raisins

- Pop everything into a little container and keep on an ice pack until ready to serve.

Rice Cracker Chips

☺ ☒ ☺ V

2 round rice cakes

- Break the rice crackers into a resealable plastic bag in rough uneven "chips."
- Serve when needed.

Squash Sticks

🍊❌🍊 V

8 ounces (250g) winter squash
1 tablespoon (15g) butter, melted
1 tablespoon pure maple syrup
½ teaspoon ground cinnamon
½ teaspoon grated nutmeg
Pinch of ground ginger

- Preheat the oven to 350°F. Line a baking sheet with parchment paper.
- Peel, seed, and cut the squash into thin sticks.
- Place on the baking sheet.
- Drizzle each stick with butter and maple syrup.
- Stir together the cinnamon, nutmeg, and ginger and sprinkle on the squash.
- Bake for 12 to 14 minutes, or until golden.
- Cool before popping into a resealable plastic bag for transportation.

Sweet Potato Cubes

⬤⬤⬤Ⓥ

4 ounces (100g) sweet potato
3 tablespoons water

- Wash, peel, and dice the sweet potato into cubes about ½ inch (1 cm) in size.
- Place the cubes in a microwave-safe dish, add the water, cover, and cook on high for 5 minutes, or until tender.
- Let them stand for 5 minutes. Pop into a sealable plastic container for transportation.
- Add a little spice by sprinkling a dash of cinnamon, nutmeg, or ginger on the sweet potato cubes.

My boys really like the sweet taste of these little morsels.
Babies have a natural sweet tooth developed from drinking
breast milk or formula, which is sweet. The natural sweetness
of sweet potatoes, squash, and many fruits make
them a favorite snack for most babies!

Teenywiches

½ avocado
2 slices bread, crusts removed
1 slice cheese

- Spread the avocado onto one slice of bread and top with the cheese.
- Add the final slice of bread and press gently.
- Cut into 9 small squares to create your teeny sandwich, and store in a sealable plastic container, ready to take anywhere.

Other suggested fillings: mashed banana, mayonnaise, and soft cheeses.

Teething Toasties

4 slices whole-grain bread, crusts removed

- Preheat the oven to 250°F.
- Cut the bread into ½-inch slices. Place on a baking sheet and bake for 1 hour.
- Allow to cool, then store in an airtight container.

BABIES WITH A COLD

If you haven't been here yet...you will, over and over and over (especially when preschool starts!). Feeding a baby with a cold can be very difficult—a loss of appetite is sometimes the first sign that a cold is on its way. Quite often, babies will refuse their food altogether if they are not feeling well. The most important thing is to make sure your baby has plenty of fluids to prevent dehydration.

Here are a few interesting ideas I have learned along the way. This next recipe, in particular, is a gem from my Nana! It's a great way to get some extra vitamins and minerals into your baby, which will boost his little immune system and help get him on the road to recovery quickly.

Chicken Soup

MAKES 4 PORTIONS

1 chicken carcass, broken apart
4 cups water, plus more as needed
1 carrot, peeled and halved
½ leek, white, light green, and dark green parts, thoroughly rinsed
1 stalk celery
Kernels cut from 1 ear of corn
2 cloves garlic, crushed
1 tablespoon vinegar
¼ cup freshly chopped parsley

- Into a large pot, place all the ingredients except the parsley.
- Bring to a boil, then reduce to a simmer.
- As the fat and scum rise to the surface, skim them off with a spoon.
- Cover and simmer for 8 hours, adding more water as needed to keep everything covered.
- Twenty minutes before the end of cooking, add the parsley.
- Remove the carcass and serve as is, or strain for a smoother broth.

My mother-in-law told me that adding a dash of vinegar to chicken soup helps extract calcium from the bones and makes the soup super nutritious.

Avocados

A wonderful way to get essential fatty acids (EFAs) into your baby! Essential fatty acids are—as their name suggests—essential to the diet because the body cannot make its own. They're the "good" fats that help the immune system recognize and fight off infections.

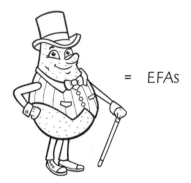 =   EFAs

Blueberries

These are a powerful immunity booster. Studies have shown that they are a great source of antioxidants.

 =   BRAINberry

Orange

Brightly colored fruits and veggies like apricots, carrots, mango, papaya, peaches, squash, and sweet potato are great sources of beta-carotene. Your baby's body converts beta-carotene to vitamin A, which helps regulate his immune system. Try using sweet potatoes in place of the white variety and mixing orange-colored fruit and veggies together in purees for double the flavor and double the protection when your baby is under the weather!

$+$ = $orange^2$

Yogurt

Yogurt is not only a great source of zinc, but it is very useful if your baby has been prescribed antibiotics, because it helps replenish the useful bacteria in his little tummy that antibiotics may destroy.

Please note: the information given here does not in any way replace professional medical advice. You should always consult a doctor if your child is unwell.

GUIDE TO GROWTH

A Baby's First Twelve Months

The first year of a baby's life is a time of astonishing change. I've seen this happen before my eyes but the facts are still amazing!

IN THE FIRST YEAR OF A BABY'S LIFE	
Month	Progress
1	Neck muscles develop for lifting head
2–3	Lifts head and neck without help Blows bubbles Smiles Coos
4	Sucks on hands Squeals
5	Pops things in mouth Begins to roll, may even roll over Starts teething Responds to own name Sits with a little support

Month	Progress
6	Sits for longer times with no support Gets into a crawl position
7	Bounces in place Holds own bottles Understands tones Begins to crawl
8	Stands and holds onto tables, sofa edges, walls, etc.
9	Understands simple questions Speaks with short words "oooh, aaah, taaa, caaar" Walks holding on to objects for support
10	Babbles Grows stronger on legs
11	Rambles Drinks and eats without help May take a couple of steps without support
12	Learns to walk without support Will have tripled his birth weight. His feet alone will reach almost half their full adult size.

FIRST FOODS FROM AROUND THE WORLD

I was doing a radio interview one day and I was asked when would be an appropriate time to introduce a baby to spices.

My reply was, "If you lived in India, it would probably be early." Then I started to wonder, what do babies around the world eat?

So I asked our global Facebook family and found the answers interesting to compare. First foods for baby in different parts of the world vary a lot. The first solid foods for some are what we would expect to find on a grown-up restaurant menu in our part of the world!

America   Oat, barley, and rice cereal; pureed vegetables; and fruit

Australia   Rice cereal, pureed vegetables and fruit

Brazil   Beans (*feijão*) of many types and colors (black, red, white)

China   *Xifan*, a rice porridge, followed by mashed fruits,
                  soft vegetables, tofu, and fish

Ghana   Maize (corn) porridge

France	Artichokes, tomatoes
India	*Khichdi*, a mushy rice-and-lentil-based dish (think a spicy, turmeric-yellow rice porridge)
Japan	Rice cereal and radish
Middle East	Hummus, baba ganoush
Mexico	Soft tortillas
New Zealand	Rice cereal, pureed sweet potato
South Africa	Maize (corn) porridge, fish
Thailand	*Khao tom* (rice soup)
United Kingdom	Rice cereal, pureed vegetables and fruit

For many cultures, an infant's first bite of solid food is ceremonial and holds religious importance. An example of this is *annaprashan*, a Hindu ritual in which the infant is fed a sweetened rice porridge which has usually been blessed by an elder family member. Similar rites of passage are practiced across Asia, including in the Bengal region, Vietnam, and Thailand.

Baby's First Menu Planner

Week 1

Day	1	2	3
Early Morning	Milk: breast or formula	Milk: breast or formula	Milk: breast or formula
Breakfast	Milk: breast or formula	Milk: breast or formula	Milk: breast or formula
Lunch	2 tsp. rice cereal + breast milk or formula	2 tsp. rice cereal + breast milk or formula	2 tsp. rice cereal + breast milk or formula
Dinner	Milk: breast or formula	Milk: breast or formula	Milk: breast or formula
Bedtime	Milk: breast or formula	Milk: breast or formula	Milk: breast or formula

4	5	6	7
Milk: breast or formula	Milk: breast or formula	Milk: breast or formula	Milk: breast or formula
Milk: breast or formula	Milk: breast or formula	Milk: breast or formula	Milk: breast or formula
Apple Puree + breast milk or formula	Apple Puree + breast milk or formula	Pear Puree + breast milk or formula	Pear Puree + breast milk or formula
Milk: breast or formula	Milk: breast or formula	Milk: breast or formula	Milk: breast or formula
Milk: breast or formula	Milk: breast or formula	Milk: breast or formula	Milk: breast or formula

Week 2

Day	1	2	3
Early Morning	Milk: breast or formula	Milk: breast or formula	Milk: breast or formula
Breakfast	Milk: breast or formula	Milk: breast or formula	Milk: breast or formula
Lunch	Apple Cream + breast milk or formula	Apple Puree + breast milk or formula	Mashed Banana + breast milk or formula
Dinner	Milk: breast or formula	Milk: breast or formula	Milk: breast or formula
Bedtime	Milk: breast or formula	Milk: breast or formula	Milk: breast or formula

4	5	6	7
Milk: breast or formula	Milk: breast or formula	Milk: breast or formula	Milk: breast or formula
Milk: breast or formula	Milk: breast or formula	Milk: breast or formula	Milk: breast or formula
Pear Puree + breast milk or formula	Orchard Fruits + breast milk or formula	Orchard Fruits + breast milk or formula	Mashed papaya + breast milk or formula
Milk: breast or formula	Milk: breast or formula	Milk: breast or formula	Milk: breast or formula
Milk: breast or formula	Milk: breast or formula	Milk: breast or formula	Milk: breast or formula

Week 3

Day	1	2	3
Early Morning	Milk: breast or formula	Milk: breast or formula	Milk: breast or formula
Breakfast	Rice cereal + breast milk or formula	Bananavo + breast milk or formula	Bananavo + breast milk or formula
Lunch	Potato + breast milk or formula	Potato Squash + breast milk or formula	Potato Squash Carrot + breast milk or formula
Dinner	Milk: breast or formula	Milk: breast or formula	Milk: breast or formula
Bedtime	Milk: breast or formula	Milk: breast or formula	Milk: breast or formula

4	5	6	7
Milk: breast or formula	Milk: breast or formula	Milk: breast or formula	Milk: breast or formula
Rice cereal + breast milk or formula	Pear Puree + breast milk or formula	Apple Cream + breast milk or formula	Banana Puree + breast milk or formula
Potato Squash Carrot + breast milk or formula	Carrot Rutabaga + breast milk or formula	Vegetable Puree + breast milk or formula	Vegetable Puree + breast milk or formula
Milk: breast or formula	Milk: breast or formula	Milk: breast or formula	Milk: breast or formula
Milk: breast or formula	Milk: breast or formula	Milk: breast or formula	Milk: breast or formula

Week 4

Day	1	2	3
Early Morning	Milk: breast or formula	Milk: breast or formula	Milk: breast or formula
Breakfast	Pear & Banana Puree + breast milk or formula	Bananavo + breast milk or formula	Bananavo + breast milk or formula
Lunch	Potato + breast milk or formula	Potato Squash + breast milk or formula	Potato Squash Carrot + breast milk or formula
Dinner	Milk: breast or formula	Milk: breast or formula	Milk: breast or formula
Bedtime	Milk: breast or formula	Milk: breast or formula	Milk: breast or formula

BABY 138 BOWL

4	5	6	7
Milk: breast or formula	Milk: breast or formula	Milk: breast or formula	Milk: breast or formula
Apple Cream + breast milk or .formula	Pear Puree + breast milk or formula	Apple Cream + breast milk or formula	Banana Puree + breast milk or formula
Potato Squash Carrot + breast milk or formula	Carrot Rutabaga + breast milk or formula	Vegetable Puree + breast milk or formula	Vegetable Puree + breast milk or formula
Milk: breast or formula	Milk: breast or formula	Milk: breast or formula	Milk: breast or formula
Milk: breast or formula	Milk: breast or formula	Milk: breast or formula	Milk: breast or formula

RESOURCES

Food allergies and intolerances
FAAN: The Food Allergy & Anaphylaxis Network
1-800-929-4040
www.foodallergy.org

National Eczema Association
Babies with eczema should always be examined by their doctor as they
are more likely to suffer from food allergies
1-800-818-7546
www.nationaleczema.org

Celiac Disease Foundation
A celiac is someone who has a severe intolerance to the gluten in wheat,
rye, barley, and oats.
1-818-990-2354
www.celiac.org

National Foundation of Celiac Awareness (NFCA)
215-325-1306
www.celiaccentral.org

Lactose Intolerance
Lactose intolerance is the inability to digest lactose, which is the sugar in
milk, due to the lack of a digestive agent called lactase in a baby's gut.
www.illinipediatrics.com/lactose_intolerance.pdf

BIBLIOGRAPHY

Books
Holford, Patrick, and Deborah Colson. *Optimum Nutrition for Your Child.* London: Piatkus Books, 2008.

Jay, Roni. *The Cook's Pocket Bible.* Devon, UK: White Ladder Press Ltd., 2006.

Kelly, Lorraine. *Baby & Toddler Eating Plan.* London: Virgin Books Ltd., 2002.

McCosker, Kim, and Rachael Bermingham. *4 Ingredients* and *4 Ingredients 2.* Caloundra, Queensland: Meymott Enterprises Pty Ltd., 2007.

Whitby, Joanna. *Practical Cooking for Babies & Toddlers.* Sydney: Choice Books, 1999.

Websites
About.com
www.babyparenting.about.com

Recipe Goldmine
www.wholesomebabyfood.com/solidfood4to6montholdbaby.htm

Introducing Solid Foods 4 to 12 months old
www.babycenter.com.au/baby/startingsolids/introducing/

Introducing Solids
www.homemade-baby-food-recipes.com/baby-food-storage

Baby Foods to Avoid
Finger Foods for Babies
www.homemade-baby-food-recipes.com

Invitation

Join our Foodie Family

At 4 Ingredients we cultivate a family of busy people all bound together by the desire to create good, healthy, homemade meals quickly, easily, and economically.

Our aim is to save one another precious time and money in the kitchen. If this is you, too, then we invite you to join our growing family where we share kitchen wisdom daily.

If you have a favorite recipe or a tip that has worked as you have raised and fed your little angels and you think others would enjoy it, please join our family at:

f : facebook.com/4ingredientspage

You Tube : 4 Ingredients Channel

www : 4ingredients.com.au

🐦 : @4ingredients

With
love and nourishment,

Kim

Index